T0198414

WestBow Press books may be ordered through booksellers or by contacting:

WestBow Press
A Division of Thomas Nelson & Zondervan
1663 Liberty Drive
Bloomington, IN 47403
www.westbowpress.com
844-714-3454

Because of the dynamic nature of the Internet, any web addresses or links contained in this book may have changed since publication and may no longer be valid. The views expressed in this work are solely those of the author and do not necessarily reflect the views of the publisher, and the publisher hereby disclaims any responsibility for them.

Any people depicted in stock imagery provided by Getty Images are models, and such images are being used for illustrative purposes only. Certain stock imagery © Getty Images.

Interior Image Credit: Reianna Barron

ISBN: 978-1-6642-7752-6 (sc)
ISBN: 978-1-6642-7754-0 (hc)
ISBN: 978-1-6642-7753-3 (e)

Library of Congress Control Number: 2022916513

Print information available on the last page.

WestBow Press rev. date: 10/18/2022

WESTBOW
PRESS®
A DIVISION OF THOMAS NELSON
& ZONDERVAN

What If My Music?

by Joel Barron

Illustrated by Reianna Barron

Acknowledgment

I want to dedicate this book to my three children: Micah, Gabriella and Jeremiah. They are my world and my reason for this book. There is power in your song that can change your circumstances. Always be willing to raise a hallelujah in the midst of the storm.

To my beautiful wife, Reianna. I am so thankful for your love and support of this project. I'm so excited that we could share in this project together to help transform the world through this positive message.

And to my family, thank you for all the encouragement and support over the years. I love you all!

What if my music

was more than a song?

What if it could pierce through darkness?

What if it could make me strong?

What if every time

a single note was played,

It soared across the heavens

and made everything okay.

What if the birds and whales could sing:

the moon, the stars,
and everything?

Could sing a song of hope and love.

Could lift their voice to God in Heaven above.

Our music can do this and so much more.

It can bring
us life, it can
bring us joy.

When we play our music,

When we sing our song,

We especially bring joy

to God above.

What if my music,

what if my song,

Was the key for
loving others

to help us
get along.